INTRODUCTION

The Intuitive Style Cleanse is here to help you develop a deeper connection with your unique style by journaling, reflecting, scrapbooking and planning.

This Style Planner is also a creative space for you to redefine and refresh your style essence.

Get ready to embark on a journey of self-exploration and personal growth as you connect with your inner voice and express yourself authentically with the help of your guided style planner.

Intuitive Style x

INTRODUCTION

CONTENTS

PAGE 01 - 05
INTRODUCTION

WEEK 1: PAGE 06-19
STYLE ESSENCE
Style Profile
Style Categories
Style Values
Style Goals

WEEK 2: PAGE 20-51
STYLE INSPIRATION
Style Likes
Style Dislikes
Style Mood Board

WEEK 3: PAGE 52-67
WARDROBE INVENTORY
Wardrobe Inventory
Gaps + Wishlist Items
Wishlist Budget Planner

INTRODUCTION

WEEK 4: PAGE 68-91
OUTFIT VISUALISATION + PLANNING

Visualise
+
Pre-plan Outfit Combinations

WEEK 5: PAGE 92-109
STYLE FORMULA

Create your unique style formula

PAGE 110-111
STYLE PLANNER COMPLETED

Congratulations On Completing
Your Styler Planner

PAGE 112-147
STYLE JOURNAL

A Writing Space To Help You
Reflect & Grow Your Style

INTRODUCTION

USING YOUR STYLE PLANNER

Before you use your style planner, we recommend you take some time to ponder on your style goals.

A clear idea of your goals will help you get the most out of your Style Planner.

For instance, you may like to experiment with new colours, patterns, trends, or outfit combinations to boost your confidence and feel more comfortable.

Remember, the most important thing is wearing what feels authentic to you.

INTRODUCTION

Your Style Planner is also an excellent tool for feeling organised and a place to explore your creativity.

Enjoy using different colour palettes, stickers, pictures, photographs and any other unique additions that will help you represent your style.

In the space below, please write down your goals for using your Style Planner.

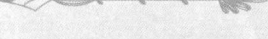

WEEK 1

STYLE ESSENCE

TAKING THE TIME TO EVALUATE YOUR
STYLE WILL HELP YOU TUNE IN WITH YOUR
UNIQUE STYLE ESSENCE

WEEK 1

QUOTE

"My heart feels free when I wear styles that inspire me."

Intuitive Style

WEEK 1

CAPTURING YOUR STYLE ESSENCE

Dressing in clothes that make you feel confident and comfortable is a powerful way to express yourself and boost your self-esteem.

Whether you prefer a minimalist look or something more eclectic, embracing your unique style essence can help you communicate your personality and values without saying a word.

As we become more conscious of the impact of our choices on the environment, sustainability has become an increasingly important factor in fashion and in expressing our style essence.

Let's celebrate our individuality, make mindful choices that make us feel good and take care of our planet.

WEEK 1

Week 1

WORKBOOK

Please complete the question-and-answer workbook.

Your week one workbook includes various sections that help identify your style profile, style categories, style goals, style values, and fashion brands.

By filling out each section thoughtfully, you'll gain valuable insights into your unique sense of style and learn how to enhance it further.

WORKBOOK

style profile

Height:

___

Shoe Size:

___

Clothing Size:

___

Eye Colour:

___

Hair Colour:

___

Face shape:

___

Body Type:

___

Skin Tone: (Warm, Neutral, Cool)

___

WORKBOOK

My Style Personality:

_____

_____

Mood:

_____

_____

Areas of my body I like to accentuate...

_____

_____

Notes:

_____

_____

_____

WORKBOOK

Create a quick list of your style goals

- [ ]
- [ ]
- [ ]
- [ ]
- [ ]
- [ ]
- [ ]
- [ ]
- [ ]
- [ ]
- [ ]
- [ ]
- [ ]

WORKBOOK

Lifestylestyle

Changing and organising your wardrobe and style can be a little overwhelming, yet taking a closer look at your lifestyle can make the process much easier.

By understanding the activities you regularly engage in, you can identify what clothing you need in your wardrobe.

Use this space to create five categories with percentages that suit your lifestyle and wardrobe needs.

Category 1	Category 2	Category 3	Category 4	Category 5
____%	____%	____%	____%	____%

For Example:
35% Everyday Wear
30% Professional Wear
20% Social Wear
5% Special Occasions
10% Active Wear

WORKBOOK

style values

How we dress conveys a message about who we are and what we stand for. Take a moment to reflect on your values and what you choose to invest in.

List four of your values...

1 _____

2 _____

3 _____

4 _____

Align your values with the clothing pieces you choose to invest in...

1 _____

2 _____

3 _____

4 _____

For Example:

"I choose to invest in clothing that compliments my body shape and skin tone."

"I choose to invest in brands that are ethical and sustainable."

"I choose to invest in quality over quantity."

"I choose to stick to my monthly clothing budget."

WORKBOOK

style environment

Aligning your sense of style with your environment can be an effective way to create a cohesive and harmonious look.

By considering your location's weather, and climate, you can make style choices that look great and are functional and comfortable.

For instance, consider prioritising breathable fabrics and lighter colours in your wardrobe if you live in a hot and humid area.

Conversely, invest in warmer outerwear and layering pieces if you live in a cooler climate.

Activities you spend most of your time doing...

1 _____

2 _____

3 _____

4 _____

Activity	Got-to outfit	Environment
1		
2		
3		
4		

WORKBOOK

style brands

Write three fashion brands that align
with your values...

    The Brand   Brand Values   Your Values

1 _____

2 _____

3 _____

What do you love about each of the fashion brands...

1 _____
_____
_____

2 _____
_____
_____

3 _____
_____
_____

WORKBOOK

Take five to ten minutes to write how you would like to communicate your style essence with the world around you without speaking...

WORKBOOK

Use this space to recap what you have learned this week...

Week One

This week, you have learned more about yourself, your style preferences, and aligning your lifestyle and wardrobe needs.

Connecting the dots between your style goals, values, and the clothing brands you choose to invest in is an insightful method to express yourself authentically.

WEEK 2

STYLE INSPIRATION

CONNECT TO YOUR CREATIVITY BY DISCOVERING THE STYLES THAT INSPIRE YOU

WEEK 2

QUOTE

"I walk barefoot in nature & find inspiration to reflect my authentic style."

Intuitive Style

WEEK 2

STYLE INSPIRATION

Exploring different styles and sources of inspiration can have numerous benefits, and it can help expand your creativity and broaden your perspective on your unique style.

By seeing how others wear different clothing pieces and mixing and matching patterns and textures, you can gain new ideas, insights, and elements that you may want to incorporate into your wardrobe.

Always keep your eyes peeled for individuals with a unique sense of style from which you can draw inspiration and add your unique twist.

Another idea is to browse fashion blogs, observe trends as you travel, or look for vibrant, inspiring outfits in magazines and on Pinterest.

WEEK 2

Week 2

WORKBOOK

Step 1
Explore the styles that you like and dislike.

STEP 2
Enjoy creating style mood boards, seasonal wear, and colour palettes that reflect your unique style.

Ensure you include inspiring hairstyles, clothing pieces, or anything that interests you.

You may like to include images from magazines, photographs, stickers, and colourful drawings to help scrapbook your style inspiration.

Step 3
Create uplifting affirmations to help you stay true to your unique style.

WORKBOOK

style likes

Exploring styles we like can help us feel more confident and comfortable in our choices. Take a moment to note the styles you feel inspired by...

Favourite Colours:

Favourite Patterns:

Favourite Textures:

WORKBOOK

Create a list of styles you like:

- [ ]
- [ ]
- [ ]
- [ ]
- [ ]
- [ ]
- [ ]
- [ ]
- [ ]
- [ ]
- [ ]
- [ ]
- [ ]
- [ ]
- [ ]
- [ ]

WORKBOOK

style dislikes

Exploring styles you dislike can help you better understand your preferences and tastes.

This can help you make more informed decisions when choosing items and making choices that reflect your style.

Take a moment to express your thoughts on styles you dislike...

_____

_____

_____

_____

_____

_____

_____

_____

_____

_____

_____

WORKBOOK

Create a list of styles you dislike:

By keeping a list of styles that don't align with your style goals, you can refer back to it when making future decisions to ensure that you stay true to your unique style.

- [ ] _____
- [ ] _____
- [ ] _____
- [ ] _____
- [ ] _____
- [ ] _____
- [ ] _____
- [ ] _____
- [ ] _____
- [ ] _____
- [ ] _____
- [ ] _____
- [ ] _____
- [ ] _____
- [ ] _____
- [ ] _____

Use this space to scrapbook your style inspiration

WORKBOOK

style mood board

style mood board

WORKBOOK

Use this space to scrapbook your style inspiration

Use this space to scrapbook your style inspiration

colour palette

style inspiration

WORKBOOK

style mood board

style inspiration

colour palette

hairstyle

favourite hairstyles

hairstyle

Use this space to scrapbook your style inspiration

favourite

WORKBOOK

Use this space to scrapbook your style inspiration

favourite

WORKBOOK

favourite

WORKBOOK

colour mood board

favourite colours chart

Autumn

the theme

_____
_____
_____
_____
_____
_____

the feeling

_____
_____
_____
_____
_____
_____

Seasonal Wardrobe

the elements

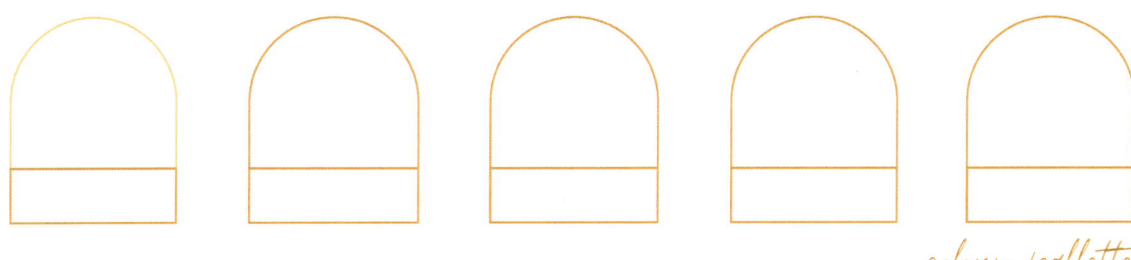

colour pallette

Spring

the theme

_____
_____
_____
_____
_____
_____

the feeling

_____
_____
_____
_____
_____
_____

WORKBOOK

Seasonal Wardrobe

the elements

_____

_____

_____

_____

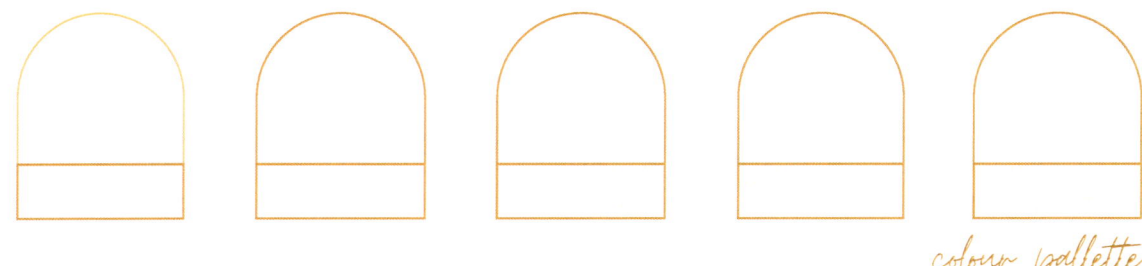

colour pallette

Summer

the theme

_____
_____
_____
_____
_____
_____
_____

the feeling

_____
_____
_____
_____
_____
_____
_____

Seasonal Wardrobe

WORKBOOK

the elements

_____

_____

_____

_____

colour pallette

Winter

the theme

_____
_____
_____
_____
_____
_____

the feeling

_____
_____
_____
_____
_____
_____

WORKBOOK

Seasonal Wardrobe

the elements

_____

_____

_____

_____

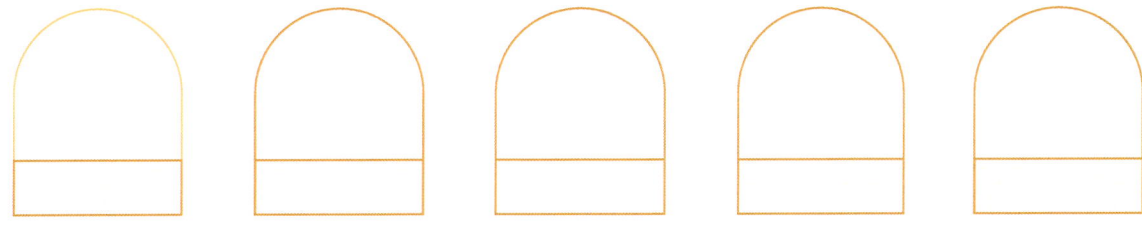

colour pallette

WORKBOOK

Style affirmations

Write affirmations that feel natural and help you feel
confident in expressing your unique style.

For example, "I am beautiful inside and out",
"I am grateful to be me."

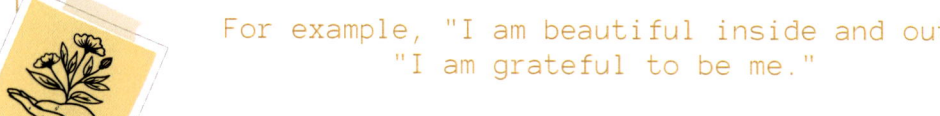

WORKBOOK

Style affirmations

Repeat the affirmations as you need them to help you stay true to your authentic style."

WORKBOOK

Use this space to recap what you have learned this week...

Week two

This week, you've discovered how exploring inspiring styles, seasonal trends, and colour palettes can broaden your knowledge of your style and help you express yourself in new and exciting ways.

Embrace the power of style inspiration to discover and showcase your unique style to the world.

WEEK 3

WARDROBE INVENTORY

TRACKING YOUR CLOTHING PIECES CAN UNLOCK THE POWER TO GET READY EFFORTLESSLY AND SAVE VALUABLE TIME

WEEK 3

QUOTE

"I dusted away the cobwebs! I re-purposed the old & gifted all that no longer served me.

Who would have known my wardrobe had all these hidden gems?"

Intuitive Style

WEEK 3

WARDROBE INVENTORY

Keeping track of the items in your wardrobe can be incredibly helpful when organising your closet.

By inventorying everything you own, you can better understand what you wear and what items you can do without.

This can help you make more informed decisions about which clothes to keep and which ones to donate, gift, recycle or sell.

Additionally, knowing what you have in your wardrobe can save you time and stress when getting dressed in the morning.

WEEK 3

Week 3

WORKBOOK

Begin the wardrobe inventory process by removing all your clothes from your wardrobe and laying them on your bed.

You can use the space in this week's workbook to list your tops, bottoms, layers, shoes, accessories, etc.

It is a good idea to keep your inventory notes up-to-date by regularly reviewing and updating them, helping you keep track of your clothing possessions.

Then, you can categorise them by colour, season, condition, brand, size and occasion.

Note any gaps and wishlist items, create a budget to help you avoid impulse purchases, and invest in pieces to enhance your wardrobe.

WORKBOOK

tops

	BRAND	SEASON	OCCASSION	COLOUR	CONDITION	SIZE
☐						
☐						
☐						
☐						
☐						
☐						
☐						
☐						
☐						
☐						
☐						
☐						
☐						
☐						
☐						
☐						
☐						

WORKBOOK

bottoms

	BRAND	SEASON	OCCASSION	COLOUR	CONDITION	SIZE
☐						
☐						
☐						
☐						
☐						
☐						
☐						
☐						
☐						
☐						
☐						
☐						
☐						
☐						
☐						
☐						
☐						
☐						

WORKBOOK

layers

	BRAND	SEASON	OCCASSION	COLOUR	CONDITION	SIZE
☐						
☐						
☐						
☐						
☐						
☐						
☐						
☐						
☐						
☐						
☐						
☐						
☐						
☐						
☐						
☐						
☐						
☐						

WORKBOOK

shoes

	BRAND	SEASON	OCCASSION	COLOUR	CONDITION	SIZE
☐						
☐						
☐						
☐						
☐						
☐						
☐						
☐						
☐						
☐						
☐						
☐						
☐						
☐	BRAND	SEASON	OCCASSION	COLOUR	CONDITION	SIZE
☐						
☐						
☐						

WORKBOOK

accessories

	BRAND	SEASON	OCCASSION	COLOUR	CONDITION	SIZE
☐						
☐						
☐						
☐						
☐						
☐						
☐						
☐						
☐						
☐						
☐						
☐						
☐						
☐						
☐						
☐						
☐						

WORKBOOK

others

	BRAND	SEASON	OCCASSION	COLOUR	CONDITION	SIZE
☐						
☐						
☐						
☐						
☐						
☐						
☐						
☐						
☐						
☐						
☐						
☐						
☐						
☐						
☐						
☐						
☐						

WORKBOOK

gaps in your wardrobe

-
-
-
-
-
-
-
-
-
-
-
-

WORKBOOK

gaps in your wardrobe

WORKBOOK

wishlist items

- ○ _____
- ○ _____
- ○ _____
- ○ _____
- ○ _____
- ○ _____
- ○ _____
- ○ _____
- ○ _____
- ○ _____
- ○ _____
- ○ _____

WORKBOOK

wishlist budget

spending allowance	

clothing items	price
total expenses	
money left over	

WORKBOOK

Use this space to recap what you have learned this week...

Week Three

This week, you have learned the value of assessing the clothing items in your wardrobe.

In the long run, it saves you time, money, and energy that you might otherwise spend shopping for unnecessary items or struggling to find something to wear.

WEEK 4

OUTFIT VISUALISATION & PLANNING

FEEL CONFIDENT AND EMPOWERED BY TAKING
THE TIME TO COORDINATE YOUR CLOTHING
PIECES AND ACCESSORIES

WEEK 4

QUOTE

"I affirm my intuitive style with my unique placement of accessories"

Intuitive Style

WEEK 4

OUTFIT VISUALISATION

Visualising your outfit combinations is an important element that can help bring your style together.

It's not just about wearing clothes that fit well and flatter your figure but also about adding the right accessories and finishing touches to elevate the overall look.

Whether it's a statement necklace, a colourful scarf, rolling up your sleeves or cuffs of your pants, layering clothing or adding a particular element to reflect the season, these small additions can make a big difference in how your outfit is perceived and how you feel.

With practice, visualising outfits can become second nature, allowing you to create unique looks that effortlessly reflect your authenticity.

WEEK 4

Week 4: step 1

WORKBOOK

OUTFIT VISUALISATION

Visualising new outfit combinations using the clothes you already have can be a powerful way to boost your creativity and bring out your confidence in your unique style.

Drawing inspiration from the style tips and ideas you've learned in previous weeks, you can create looks that truly reflect who you are.

Sometimes, the best outfits are the ones that come together naturally without overthinking it.

Take a moment to trust your instincts, imagine six new combinations in your wardrobe, and let your imagination run wild.

Remember to document your journey in the workbook section.

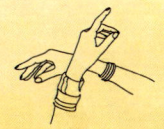

WORKBOOK

Style Ideas:
_____
_____
_____

Season/Weather:
_____
_____
_____

The Occasion:
_____
_____
_____

Style Additions:
_____
_____

The Feeling:
_____

Style Ideas:

_____

_____

_____

Season/Weather:

_____

_____

_____

The Occassion:

_____

_____

_____

Style Additions:

_____

_____

_____

The Feeling:

_____

_____

_____

outfit combination ideas

WORKBOOK

Style Ideas:

_____

_____

_____

Season/Weather:

_____

_____

_____

The Occasion:

_____

_____

_____

Accessories:

_____

_____

Style Additions:

_____

_____

The feeling:

_____

_____

WORKBOOK

outfit combination ideas

Style Ideas:

_____

_____

_____

Season/Weather:

_____

_____

_____

The Occasion:

_____

_____

_____

Accessories:

_____

_____

_____

Extra Additions:

_____

_____

_____

The Feeling:

_____

_____

WORKBOOK

The Look:

outfit combination ideas

The Look:

WEEK 4

OUTFIT PLANNING

Now that you have visualised style combinations, it's time to plan new outfit combinations for different occasions.

It not only saves you time but can also help boost your confidence and self-esteem.

Planning your outfits eliminates the hassle of last-minute decisions and ensures you are dressed appropriately for the occasion.

It also allows you to mix and match your clothing items, creating new outfits and getting the most out of your wardrobe.

If your clothing pieces don't align with how you want to express your authentic style, you can start by picking a few of your favourite items and brainstorming ways to enhance their look.

WEEK 4

Week 4: step 2

WORKBOOK

1. Create outfit combinations for occasions special to you with the clothing in your wardrobe.

You can refer to your wardrobe inventory and pair items to see what looks good.

2. You may like to try your new outfit combinations on to see what pairs well together or lay them flat on the bed, take pictures of each outfit combination, save them on your phone or computer, and consider printing them for later reference.

3. Then, document your complete outfit combinations in the workbook.

WORKBOOK

In week one of your workbook, you created five categories to reflect your lifestyle and wardrobe needs.

You can use the chart below to reflect the categories and percentages you created in week one.

Example

% Everyday Wear

% Professional Wear

% Social Wear

% Special Occasions

% Active Wear

WORKBOOK

Create a list of up to eight occasions for which you would like to pre-plan outfits...

○ _____

○ _____

○ _____

○ _____

○ _____

○ _____

○ _____

○ _____

Please document and go into detail about each of your outfits in this weeks workbook.

WORKBOOK

outfit #1

Occassion:

Season/Weather

Top:

Bottoms:

Shoes:

Accessories:

Layers/Other:

WORKBOOK

outfit #2

Occassion:

Season/Weather

Top:

Bottoms:

Shoes:

Accessories:

Layers/Other:

WORKBOOK

outfit #3

Occassion:
_____

Season/Weather
_____

Top:
_____

Bottoms:
_____

Shoes:
_____

Accessories:
_____

Layers/Other:
_____

WORKBOOK

outfit #4

Occassion:

Season/Weather

Top:

Bottoms:

Shoes:

Accessories:

Layers/Other:

WORKBOOK

outfit #5

Occassion:
_____

Season/Weather
_____

Top:
_____

Bottoms:
_____

Shoes:
_____

Accessories:
_____

Layers/Other:
_____

WORKBOOK

outfit #6

Occassion:

Season/Weather

Top:

Bottoms:

Shoes:

Accessories:

Layers/Other:

WORKBOOK

outfit #1

Occassion:
_____

Season/Weather
_____

Top:
_____

Bottoms:
_____

Shoes:
_____

Accessories:
_____

Layers/Other:
_____

WORKBOOK

outfit #1

Occassion:
___

Season/Weather
___

Top:
___

Bottoms:
___

Shoes:
___

Accessories:
___

Layers/Other:
___

WORKBOOK

Use this space to recap what you have learned this week...

Week Four

This week, you have learned how to organise and enjoy a creative approach to your style.

Outfit visualising and planning can be a fun and creative way to express yourself and showcase your unique personality through your style choices.

By taking the time to visualise and plan out your outfits in advance, you can save time, reduce stress, and make more use of your existing wardrobe.

WEEK 5

STYLE FORMULA

CONFIDENTLY EXPRESS YOUR AUTHENTIC STYLE WITH
EASE AND CONSISTENCY WITH YOUR UNIQUE FORMULA

WEEK 5

QUOTE

"Today, I'm expressing
my authenticity.
Be bold, be free!"

Intuitive Style

WEEK 5

STYLE FORMULA

Refining your style formula can unlock the power to effortlessly showcase your unique style and build a wardrobe that truly reflects who you are again and again.

Creating a clear style formula empowers you to curate a collection of pieces that bring you joy and help you feel confident.

With determination and focus, you can achieve a wardrobe that reflects your inner self and radiates confidence, bringing joy and inspiration to your daily life.

WEEK 5

WORKBOOK

Use this week's workbook space to envision your Style Formula.

Use words, quotes and pictures to illustrate your clear style formula vision.

WORKBOOK

Please write a note to yourself to help you feel empowered to express your unique style.

style formula

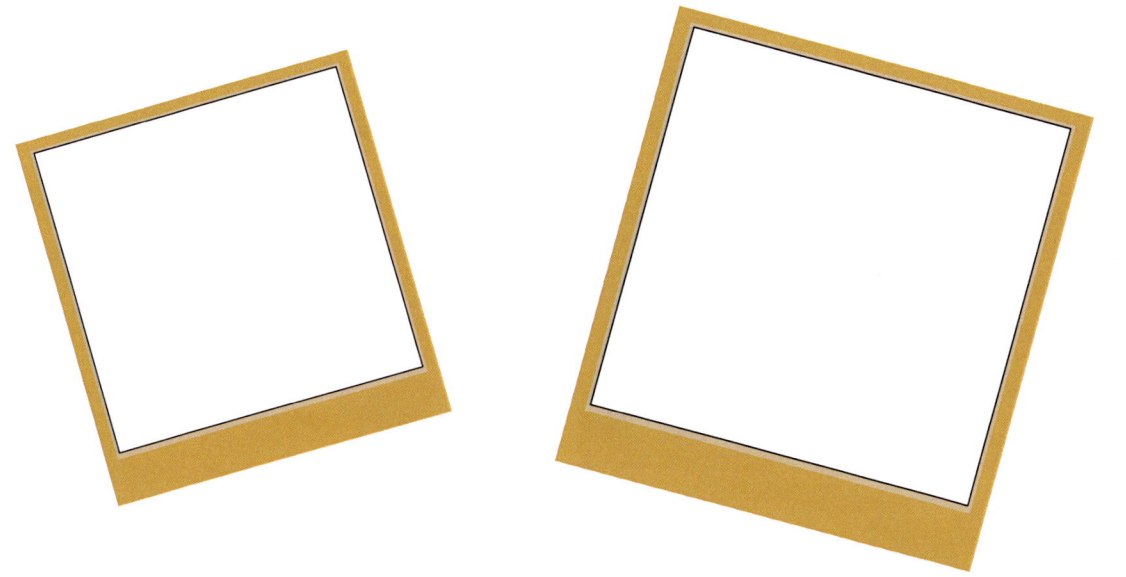

WORKBOOK

inspirational quotes + words

style formula

WORKBOOK

the Look

colour inspiration

the activity

words that describe my style

style inspiration

style formula

style inspiration

the Look

colour inspiration

the Activity

words that describe my style

WORKBOOK

style inspiration

the activity

the Look

the feeling

words that describe my style

_____

_____

_____

colour inspiration

style formula

style inspiration

the activity

the look

words that describe my style

the feeling

colour inspiration

WORKBOOK

the Look

colour inspiration

the activity

words that describe my style

style inspiration

style formula

style inspiration

colour inspiration

the Look

the activity

words that describe my style

_____

_____

_____

WORKBOOK

style inspiration

the activity

the look

the feeling

words that describe my style

colour inspiration

style formula

style inspiration

the activity

the Look

the feeling

words that describe my style

_____

_____

_____

colour inspiration

WORKBOOK

How your style formula inspires you...

Week Five

Over the past five weeks, you have gained insight to help you express your style essence.

Your commitment to exploring your style inspiration and documenting and planning your outfits has helped you create a formula aligned with your unique style.

CONGRATULATIONS

Congratulations on completing the Style Planner Workbook and Guide.

Your dedication to improving your style and confidence and tuning into your style essence is genuinely inspiring, and the knowledge and skills you have acquired through this journey will undoubtedly benefit you.

Stay committed to your self-love and style journey, and keep expanding as you grow in confidence.

Throughout the five weeks of your Style Planner, you have unlocked the power of your unique style.

Once again, congratulations on this incredible accomplishment!

Intuitive Style x

As you turn the page, you'll find your Style Journal. This space is here to help you connect, reflect and grow your unique style with any changes. Xx

STYLE JOURNAL

STYLE JOURNAL

MAKE THE MOST OF THIS JOURNAL-WRITING SPACE BY
REFLECTING AS YOUR STYLE GROWS

STYLE JOURNAL

QUOTE

"I encourage myself & the world around me by wearing styles that enlighten me."

'Intuitive Style'

STYLE JOURNAL

STYLE JOURNAL

Our unique style evolves and changes with us as we journey through life.

It's a beautiful thing to witness this growth and embrace the transformation.

Allow yourself to enjoy the process of evolving your style, and turn a page in this journal space for reflection and growth.

style journal *date*

the way I feel when I express my unique style

style journal *date*

The kind of message I would like my style to convey is...

three words that describe my style are...

style journal

date

are there any areas of my wardrobe I need to improve or update?

style + wardrobe layout inspiration

style journal

date

I feel...

style journal date

119

style journal

date

my favourite outfit this month is...

expressing my unique style helps me...

the positive emotions I feel when I express my unique style...

style journal   date

I feel most confident when...

my style mood this month is...

recent compliments people have given me about my style

reflecting on my wardrobe & style...

style journal   *date*

the best places to find style inspiration is...

new colours I'd like to experiment with in my wardrobe are...

styles and trends I'm drawn to...

style journal — *date*

style trends I'd like to try

colours and fabrics I feel most confident and comfortable in...

fabrics I prefer...

style journal

date

I am...

style journal

date

style journal *date*

the way I feel when I express my unique style

style journal *date*

style journal

date

the kind of message I would like my style to convey is...

three words that describe my style are...

style journal *date*

are there any areas of my wardrobe I need to improve or update?

style + wardrobe layout inspiration

style journal   date

I feel....

how can I incorporate new elements into my style while staying true to myself...

areas of my wardrobe I want to improve or update ...

style journal   Date

the styles & trends I'm drawn to are...

the colours and patterns I feel most confident and comfortable in...

the fabrics I prefer are...

133

style journal *date*

my favourite outfit this month is...

expressing my unique style helps me...

the positive emotions I feel when I express my unique style...

… # style journal

date

I feel most confident when…

my style mood this month is…

recent compliments people have given me about my style

reflecting on my wardrobe & style...

style journal *date*

the best places to find style inspiration is...

new colours I'd like to experiment with in my wardrobe are...

styles and trends I'm drawn to...

style journal

date

style trends I'd like to try...

colours and patterns I feel most confident and comfortable in...

fabrics I prefer...

style journal

date

I feel...

how can I incorporate new elements into my style while staying true to myself...

areas of my wardrobe I want to improve or update...

style journal

Date

the styles & trends I'm drawn to are...

the colours and patterns I feel most confident and comfortable in...

the fabrics I prefer are...

style journal

date

the way I feel when I express my unique style

style journal

date

143

style journal　　　　　　　　　　　　　　　　　　　　　　　　　　　　　*date*

the kind of message I would like my style to convey is....

three words that describe my style are...

style journal *date*

are there any areas of my wardrobe I need to improve or update?

style + wardrobe layout inspiration

style journal

date

style journal   *date*

STAY IN TOUCH

IF YOU'D ENJOY CONNECTING WITH ME ON SOCIAL MEDIA, YOU CAN FIND ME ON INSTAGRAM:

@INTUITIVE.STYLE

IF YOU LOVE YOUR 'STYLE JOURNAL', FEEL FREE TO SHARE THE LOVE AND TAG ME IN YOUR SOCIAL POST.

FIND MORE STYLE AND WARDROBE CLEANSE INSPIRATION AT WWW.INTUITIVESTYLE.CO

your style aligned series
first edition

BY CHANDRA-LUCINDA, FOUNDER OF INTUITIVE STYLE

IMAGE CONSULTANT | CONTENT CREATOR | STYLE + SELF-LOVE RITUALS

AUSTRALIA

COPYRIGHT

© 2023 BY INTUITIVE STYLE
ALL RIGHTS RESERVED

www.ingramcontent.com/pod-product-compliance
Lightning Source LLC
Chambersburg PA
CBRC092341290426
44109CB00009B/178